Rebuilding the City of
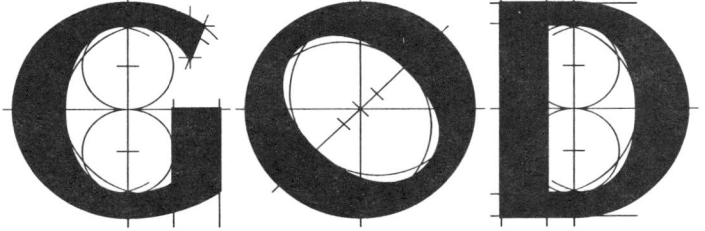

Rebuilding the City of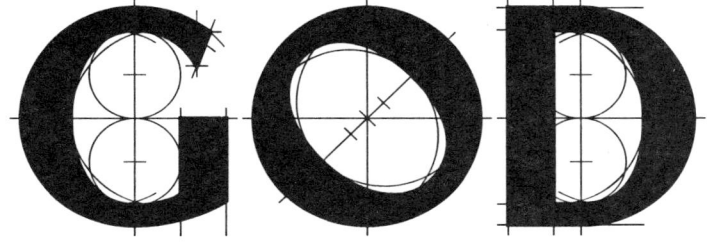

An Ancient Leader Challenges the 21st Century Church

Bill Henegar

Copyright © 1999
Covenant Publishing Company

Printed and Bound in the
United States of America
All Rights Reserved

International Standard Book Number: 1-892435-02-0

*To three leaders
who have deeply blessed my life:
T. J. Walling
Howard A. White
M. Norvel Young*

ACKNOWLEDGMENTS

It is always humbling, as we complete any work, to reflect back on how dependent on others we are to accomplish important tasks. When it comes to publishing a book, there are many people involved in the endeavor — from encouragement and advice to proofreading and editing.

I am indebted to my associate, Joyce Hutchison, for her assistance in reading the manuscript and offering her corrections and suggestions. And I appreciate the help of my friend, Professor F. LaGard Smith, whose candid comments made me see that my original work needed to be rewritten and improved. My brother-in-law, Lynn Hamm, and my brother, Ron Henegar, both read the manuscript for content and encouraged me to proceed when I wondered about the value in the leadership principles I wanted to describe.

A special word of thanks to my colleague, Dr. Jerry Rushford, the consummate promoter, who finds ways to press projects through to completion — who is a great encourager and believer in the work of his friends.

A debt of gratitude goes to Edwin White, a dear brother in the Lord, and Dr. Jameso Fuzzell, a patron of good works, both of Covenant Publishing for seeing something in this manuscript worth printing.

As always, my wife, Laurette, sustains my work and my life. I owe her everything.

CONTENTS

Introduction   11

1 Departure   15

2 Spirit   17

3 Character   35

4 Strategy   51

5 Process   65

6 The N Factor   81

Outline   91

INTRODUCTION
As you begin . . .

In the pages that follow, a story is presented that forms the framework for communicating certain concepts. The primary purpose of this fantasy is not simply to tell a tale, but to use the narrative as a device that will introduce important leadership principles — approaches that may help us to be more effective leaders today.

The basis for this narrative is the Book of Nehemiah in the Old Testament. In that document, a man named Nehemiah tells of receiving word that Jerusalem, his ancestral home, had been destroyed and all its inhabitants scattered and humiliated. Nehemiah himself was serving the Persian king, Artaxerxes, as an officer (cupbearer) in the royal court at Susa.

Nehemiah was descended from those Jews who were carried into Babylonian captivity by Nebuchadnezzar around 581 BC. When Babylon was overthrown by Cyrus the Persian in 539 BC, many of the enslaved Jews were allowed to return home. However, as we discover from Nehemiah, the returning former exiles were unsuccessful in wresting Jerusalem and the vicinity from the neighboring hostile nations. Upon hearing of the situation in

REBUILDING THE CITY OF GOD

about 444 BC, Nehemiah obtained permission from King Artaxerxes to travel to Jerusalem and lead a rebuilding and repopulation program.

Nehemiah's phenomenal success as leader and governor is good reason to revisit this great man of God and to analyze the qualities in his life and the techniques that empowered him to revitalize a defeated people.

It may be helpful to read the biblical account if you are unfamiliar with the details of the story. On the other hand, you probably will be able to read between the lines and generally understand the background of Nehemiah's struggles and triumphs from this fanciful story. In either case, the narrative itself is not the key, and I urge you not to be preoccupied with it. It is *Nehemiah's leadership principles* that may have the potential to revive and revolutionize people and institutions today, and it is those principles that should be carefully considered.

A final note: After I originally drafted this manuscript, I set it aside for a few months as I often do with my writing. I like to see if the ideas and words hold up over time. When I picked up the manuscript later, I decided it needed some fairly extensive revision. After that, I set it aside once again. More than a year went by before I next read it, but by then the ideas and words seemed simplistic, and I worried that the project would never be received the way I had accepted and been moved by the life and leadership of Nehemiah.

Every principle seemed so self-evident and elementary. However, as I laid the principles beside the events of that year at the church where I served as a leader, I realized that I and the other leaders had fallen short of nearly every one of these principles. And I

INTRODUCTION

thought, "If these things are so basic that they need not be expressed, then why are we failing in most of them?" And I thought of other churches and other leaders, and again it occurred to me that, as simple as these principles are, they are desperately needed in church after church after church.

So I ask that you resist the temptation to say, "Oh, I know all that!" And instead, look at the principles with fresh eyes. Each chapter ends with a set of questions — three per principle — which should aid in using this story as a small group study, or for personal meditation. Most or all of these questions need to be asked over and over through the months and years. Conversely, they are not such that, once answered, they can be forgotten.

Leadership is a growth process, and all who aspire to participate with God in leading His people must patiently strive to improve themselves by His grace. They will continue to press on — to succeed where they have fallen before. Perhaps Nehemiah's life and leadership can be replicated today — in you. And perhaps the challenge of this ancient leader will revitalize your ministry . . . to the praise of God's glorious grace.

> Bill Henegar
> Thousand Oaks, California

1
DEPARTURE

Suppose you and I have been chosen for a great adventure. We are part of a time-travel project team, and we are preparing for an expedition back to the fifth century before Christ, to Jerusalem in ancient Judea. There, we will not only experience a slice of history, but we will have the opportunity of interviewing and studying the great builder and leader of God's people, Nehemiah.

Our destination is a puzzle to some people. They wonder why this place and this particular time period have been selected. And why Nehemiah has been chosen as a case study. Why not Socrates or Alexander the Great or Julius Ceasar? Indeed, even in that given time period, why not examine the life of the Persian king, Artaxerxes, Nehemiah's master, who was a powerful ruler of a large empire?

Certainly, Nehemiah was a minor leader in the history of a rather minor people. The Hebrews were never a real world power. That is why it is so curious that they should impact history as profoundly as they have. What small nation is still studied with such regularity and intensity today as the Children of Israel? Likewise, Nehemiah's

REBUILDING THE CITY OF GOD

role in Hebrew history is very narrow when compared with Samuel, David, Solomon, Elijah or other leaders.

And yet, as people search for models of effective, biblical leadership, Nehemiah's success becomes a shining example for us. And perhaps our choice of time period and case study is vindicated.

Leadership in our age is characterized by a struggle for power, just as it is in every age. But the leadership of Nehemiah is strikingly different. He assumed just enough power to accomplish his task, then he willingly laid that power aside as the task was completed.

What do you suppose Nehemiah would tell us about the elements of leadership if we could interview him today? What would he say is basic to godly leadership? And what were the qualities that seemed to set him apart as a great leader? These are the things we want to discover as we travel through space and time, as we seek an audience with Governor Nehemiah.

Our time vehicle is ready. What it looks like and how it works is not important. What is important is that it will transport us to Jerusalem — somewhere around 444 B.C.

We strap ourselves inside and prepare for the journey. The controls are set. The computers, circuits and mechanisms whir into motion. There is a blinding flash and a deafening sound. Then the roar trails off into an eerie silence.

2
SPIRIT

The hatch slowly swings open. We cautiously climb out of the vehicle and step into a somehow familiar, yet strange world.

Just a mile or two away is the city, with its famous walls intact! Apparently Nehemiah has already completed much of his celebrated task. We enter the city gate and, in our best ancient Hebrew, ask directions to the governor's residence.

When we reach the house in the upper city, we request an audience with Nehemiah. Since there are still enemies in the region, we are searched and questioned by guards. Satisfied that we are not a threat and that we simply want to interview the governor about the rebuilding of Jerusalem, they lead us down a long hall. At the end of the hallway, we enter a room where daylight streams in through slits in the wall facing the courtyard.

We hardly have time to look around the room when a man appears in the doorway. He stands there silently for a moment, as if he is evaluating us. When he is satisfied that everything is in order, he enters the room.

REBUILDING THE CITY OF GOD

"Please be welcome in my house," says the man in a soft but assured voice. "I am Nehemiah. How may I help you?"

We are not prepared for the image before us. "Could this really be Nehemiah?" we think. "He should be taller, more muscular, more handsome. This man looks like one of the shopkeepers or produce vendors — maybe he has a bit more formal bearing — but he's certainly not very charismatic looking."

Yet there he is: Standing before us is a man greatly admired by many, whose ancient words have been read and studied countless times . . . a man who has been dead for more than 2,400 years. Or rather, we won't be born for another 2,400 years!

The irony overwhelms us as we simply say, "Sir, we have come a great, great distance because of our respect for you as a leader. We have come to learn about leadership from you, if you will be gracious enough to teach us."

Nehemiah motions for us to be seated. We ease down on two finely embroidered pillows as an assistant places cups of wine on the low table. The governor chooses a spot on the other side of the table and seats himself.

Again in our best Hebrew, we say, "It is an honor to meet you, Governor Nehemiah."

He smiles faintly. "It is obvious that you are foreigners. Why is it so important that you meet with me? Who told you of our building project?"

"Your fame — and that of your builders — has spread afar," we reply. "Jews in many places are telling of

SPIRIT

the great thing that God has done through His people. We want to carry details of the rebuilding of Jerusalem to God's people everywhere. But above all, we want to understand how you were able to lead such a remarkable work. In fact, we want to learn how we ourselves might become leaders and rebuilders of God's people in other places."

"You may ask me any question you like," Nehemiah responds, "and I will do my best to answer you truly."

It is time to go to work. We pull out a pad and pen and get ready to take down notes.

"Sir, our first and most basic question is, How did you go about leading a defeated people to rebuild the walls of Jerusalem? What were the various elements of this great work?"

Nehemiah stares at the strange pad of paper and the ballpoint pen. Finally he looks up and says, "That is not an easy question to answer. By 'elements,' I assume that you do not mean the elements of stone and wood. You mean the methods, the plans, even the attitudes I had as we built the City of God."

We nod.

The governor looks away thoughtfully for a moment then says, "You must understand that I never planned to be a leader. I have no formal training in leadership from royal lineage or noble family. Neither am I an architect or builder. I am only a servant. That is all. For most of my life I have been the cupbearer to King Artaxerxes of Persia."

"Yes, sir, we have heard that," we reply.

REBUILDING THE CITY OF GOD

Nehemiah continues. "But since you appear to have come so far, I will tell you what I can. First, what you see around you — these newly built walls, these strong gates — are the work of Almighty God. Far more than the labor of many people, much less the cleverness of one man, this is of our God. He encouraged us, He strengthened us, He defeated our enemies. Human effort alone will fail, but with God, we *do not* fail."

The governor pauses, then looks directly at us. "But of course, God lifts up those who call on His Name. So I will tell you what I can about how to be not just a leader, but a *godly* leader. And I will begin with this statement, which may appear rather simple and self-evident:

SPIRIT

*A godly leader must be
a "special kind of person"
with a "special kind of plan."*

"Now, I realize that is a very general and obvious statement, so I will explain to you what I mean by it. First, I will describe what I have in mind when I say **special kind of person.**

"There are two unseen elements that have to do with being that special person. And those elements are *Spirit* and *Character.*

"Let us begin with the element I call **Spirit** — considering the things that make someone a 'spiritual person,' whether that person is a leader or not.

"A spiritual person is, above all, a person of faith, specifically someone who is moved by the Spirit of God. However, to me, that means more than simply being sensitive to 'spiritual things' — or even acknowledging the existence of the Lord God. I am sure you will agree that Satan has no choice but to acknowledge God's existence — even while he remains defiant to God's will. No, I believe a godly leader is one who has a much deeper faith than that. The first attribute is:

1.
A leader has complete dependence on God.

"This humble building project is not a remarkable achievement when compared to the glorious capitals of the world's great empires. But believe me, it was impossible from a human standpoint because of my lack of knowledge and ability and because of the lack of power and courage of the people. From the very moment

SPIRIT

God put it into my heart to return here, I *trusted Him* to do what was impossible. Most leaders I have known depend upon their own abilities and the abilities of their armies, their wisemen and their workers. But I *completely depended upon God* to lead us and defend us. My understanding of faith is: placing complete trust in God and believing that He can, if He wills, do the impossible."

Nehemiah stops for a moment as we jot down our notes. Then the governor begins again.

"I remember the moment well. When I heard of the terrible situation of the city of my fathers, my heart fell. I was absolutely distraught. You see, though I lived in one world, my heart was in another. My home is in Susa, far away in Persia, but my roots are here in the Judean hills. Jerusalem is the home of my heart. My deepest loyalties are to God and to His people . . . and to His Holy City, as a symbol of the fathers and the covenants. So I was unbearably grieved."

We speak up. "Sir, we understand what you said about trust and dependence, but do you think your grief over Jerusalem had anything to do with the spiritual part of being a leader?"

"Be patient," says Nehemiah. "That is what I am about to explain. I felt deeply about the situation here in Jerusalem because of my allegiance to God and His people. When the Lord God and the children of Israel are in disgrace, then I am in disgrace as well. When I heard the news of the condition of the Jews and the city, I immediately prayed to the Lord and confessed the sins of the people — and *my own sins* and the sins of my entire family. For several days, I fasted and prayed, asking God

REBUILDING THE CITY OF GOD

to bring His people back to the place He had given them . . . to Jerusalem, even as He had promised in ages past.

"So first, a leader must have the kind of faith in God that I have described," he continues. "Then, the second attribute of a spiritual leader is penitence, godly sorrow. Perhaps I can call it 'brokenness.' You see, God's true leaders in the past were those who called the people back to the Lord. It is our nature to drift away from the Almighty. And messengers — godly leaders — are graciously sent to restore the way of those of us who have gone astray. So, if we understand 'broken walls' in a spiritual sense, we can say:

2.
A leader begins rebuilding broken walls by having a broken heart.

"What I mean is, Jerusalem was destroyed because of the pride, the disobedience, the faithlessness of the people. And one cannot rebuild a wall that has been broken because of sin without facing and confessing those sins that were the cause. We must always understand that the real tragedy is not simply a destroyed city — a heap of rubble, stones, ash, or even a destroyed people — but, rather, what that destruction represents: *broken covenants* with the God of heaven. Spirit and character work hand in hand in a leader, and an important part of character is honesty. Here is an example. If we are not honest about the situation of God's people and about our own situation — if we deny that something is terri-

SPIRIT

bly wrong — then we will never experience the broken heart that precedes the beginning of repair.

"The beginning of repairs for a broken wall is bowing low, *humbling ourselves* before our Mighty God and repenting of our sins."

We nod in agreement and scribble on our pad of paper. We add the concept of **brokenness** to the attribute of **trust.**

The governor begins again. "Now I will give you a third characteristic of the spiritual person, and it involves the force behind our actions."

"Force behind our actions?" we interrupt. "Sir, do you mean motivation?"

"'Motivation?' Is that what you would call it?" Nehemiah responds. "Nevertheless, a spiritual person completely depends upon God and is broken in spirit. But it takes *even more than those two things* to move us into action:

3.
A leader has deep reverence for God.

"I often pray and meditate before my God. And as I do, my reverence for Him stirs deep within me. I fear His power and majesty because He is so very far above me and above all things. Do you understand this idea of the holiness of God?"

We are stunned for a second at the direct question.

"Uh . . . uh, yes," we finally manage. "We have an idea of what holiness is, sir."

The governor continues. "Well, I revere the Holy God with all my heart. I respect Him and love Him because He has come near to me, to all of us, in mercy. And He has not despised us because of our weaknesses. It is that love and desire to please the Holy God, mixed with awe and a dread of His displeasure, that moves me to action. The only way I can remain *unmoved* to action is to *not* think about my love and fear of the Most High. So you see, this reverence is quite different from the dependence and brokenness I spoke of."

The governor smiles and says, "Forgive my many words — we really should be more attentive to the words of God and limit our own pronouncements. Do you not agree?"

Without waiting for a reply, he rushes on. "In fact, that brings me to another attribute of the spiritual leader . . . one that is similar to this reverence we are discussing. A leader trusts God, is sensitive to personal sinfulness, and stands in awe of Him, but also:

4.
A leader has a thirst for God's Word.

"I do not know what it was like in the days of Moses or Joshua or Samuel. Or in the time of the Kings. That was long ago. But I can tell you that after God's people were taken away in defeat to a foreign land, when

SPIRIT

we of the Exile returned to Jerusalem and heard the Holy Scriptures read aloud, we *wept* . . . we wept openly. It was a profound moment that I shall never forget as long as I live. Because God had spoken to us in His Word.

"*God has spoken.* Do you know what it means to say that? *GOD* has spoken!" He shouts the words.

Then, more quietly, "And we, His people, should be like earthen vessels, thirsty mouths opened wide to receive the water of His Word. May He ever fill us to overflowing!"

The governor pauses and closes his eyes. We wonder what is going on in the leader's mind. But in a moment Nehemiah's eyes are open again, roaming the recesses of the ceiling and the corners of the room, as if he is looking for the right words there.

"And so," he finally continues, "God's leader is like a traveler in the desert, dying of thirst, scanning the horizon for an oasis where there might be a few drops of precious water. Except that God's leader is one who thirsts for even the slightest word that falls from the mouth of the Lord God. The leader knows that without the Word of God, we are lost in a thick darkness. We are undone. But in His Word, we walk in bright sunlight."

Nehemiah suddenly straightens up and stretches. "You listen carefully, my friends, and you seem to hear even my unspoken thoughts."

The governor rises to his feet. "Come, let us walk," he says. "It will help us to think more clearly."

REBUILDING THE CITY OF GOD

We emerge from the stone building, closely followed by a bodyguard composed of four strong warriors. The governor points in the direction of the Temple, and the small entourage moves up the cobblestone street with Nehemiah slightly ahead.

The great leader is reflective as we walk. "I remember those terrible days after my brother Hanani and the other men came to Susa and I learned of the fate of my countrymen and Jerusalem." He looks to his left and right, then continues, "As I prayed and fasted, God seemed to *put it in my heart* to return to His city and rebuild its walls."

Nehemiah stops short and turns. "Mind you, I did not hear the Word of God directly, as Moses did. But the message was there in my heart nonetheless: 'Go,' God seemed to say. From my own experience and from the record of the Scrolls, I truly believe every leader of God should hear some kind of call from the Lord. A godly leader is *not a volunteer,* you know, offering service of which one may boast. Instead, God's leader is a person **chosen and called** by God Himself, a person under orders. Someone called by the God of heaven has only two choices in life: obey or not obey."

The governor's voice grows stronger, and he raises a clinched fist as he remembers the moment. "I could avoid it only if I ignored my God," he says with emotion. "Again the call came within my heart — 'Go and call My people to the work!'"

Nehemiah turns and walks at a slower pace. "I can tell you," he continues, "that both sadness and fear gripped my heart as I next entered the presence of King Artaxerxes. Of course, he noticed my countenance, my 'sadness of heart,' as he called it.

SPIRIT

"Though my throat was tight with fear, I said, 'May the king live forever. Why should my face not look sad when the city where my fathers are buried lies in ruins, and its gates have been destroyed by fire?' You understand, do you not, that my countenance in the presence of the king could have doomed me?

"Well, I prayed silently to the Lord all through the conversation. And God was with me, always moving ahead of me. I am sure it was He who opened the king's heart. I was allowed to come to Jerusalem and rebuild this city . . . and call the people back to God."

As we walk, we add to the list of spiritual qualities:

5.
A leader is faithful in communicating with God.

We notice how often Nehemiah speaks of prayer. It should be obvious that a leader among God's people must be a person of frequent and passionate prayer. But apparently it is not always so obvious. Many leaders seem to pray only occasionally.

As we think of the governor's unusual mannerisms at times, it occurs to us that the pauses in Nehemiah's conversations are probably punctuations of prayer. And we consider how often people look for leaders who are clever and who have business sense rather than leaders who have a life distinguished by communion and communication with God!

REBUILDING THE CITY OF GOD

Nehemiah stops and points to his left. From where we stand we can view a large portion of the northwest section of Jerusalem.

"As you can see," says the governor, "we are slowly repopulating the city. It has taken a great amount of work — and courage — on the part of the people to reach this point. And we are not nearly finished. It would have been easiest to have left the people alone, to have left them in their little villages and towns. But I do not believe that is what God wanted. Jerusalem is *His* city. It is the city of His Temple. Our fathers lived and died here, are buried here. God's people were in great disgrace. How did this make God feel?"

After a moment of silence, we look toward the governor, who obviously is waiting for us to respond to the not-so-rhetorical question. Again caught off guard, we stammer, "Well, uh, God must have been disappointed, sad, perhaps even angry."

"Yes," the governor says very quietly. "And His Name was diminished among the nations, because His people reflect on His reputation. I think I felt something of that same reproach. That mutual feeling with God, becoming one with the Lord God in purpose, in heart, in will, moved me to do something . . . to step out and lead."

Quickly, we jot down a sixth characteristic:

6.
A leader identifies with God and His purposes.

SPIRIT

Meanwhile, the governor continues. "Regardless of who or what is on the *other* side, I have pledged to be on *God's* side, united with Him in every way that I can be. He is holy, high and lifted up, far beyond me in every way. But I must try to understand what is vital and important to Him. I must try to embrace His feelings, His purposes, His will."

Nehemiah turns and walks on. The rest of the entourage quickly catches up with him. He walks with his hands clasped behind him, his head slightly bowed.

"I will give you one last spiritual characteristic of the godly leader," he says. "And it is a quality that flows out of the previous one. As a leader tries to embrace the feelings, purposes and will of God, there is one central attribute of God that must be emulated. Though a person has all the other qualities I have mentioned, if this last one is missing, then that person is not the kind of leader God looks for. You see:

7.
A leader has a passion for God's people.

"You may remember," the governor continues, "that when our father Abraham discovered that God was planning to destroy Sodom and Gomorrah, he negotiated with the Lord. He entreated Him — bargained with Him, we might say — asking that Sodom be spared if 50 righteous people could be found in the city. Pressing farther, Abraham asked God if He would spare the city if only 45 righteous could be found; then he dropped the number to

REBUILDING THE CITY OF GOD

40, then 30, then 20, and finally 10. And God agreed that He would not destroy Sodom if even only 10 righteous people could be found in the city. So you see, Abraham interceded for the people, not wishing that the city be destroyed.

"You also may remember that God became furious with the Israelites and their rebellion in making the golden calf at Mount Sinai. When He said He would destroy them all and make a nation of Moses, Moses entreated the Lord on behalf of the people. He reasoned with God, and God seemed to change His mind.

"Both of these great leaders had a bond with the people; an unbreakable cord of love united them. So much so that Abraham and Moses risked their very lives interceding before the Lord, appearing before an angry God to plead the case of the people — which was hardly a case at all. These leaders had a passion for God's people. And I say to you that every person who dares to lead must have that same love for people and oneness with them.

"In my view," Nehemiah concludes, "these are some of the most important spiritual characteristics of a godly leader."

We drink in every word from the governor. We have embarked upon a journey in search of leadership principles, and even at this early moment, we are not disappointed.

SPIRIT

Reflections on What It Means to Be a *Special Kind of Person:*

The Spirit Component

1. What are some signs that a person may not really be depending on God?
2. What is the difference between casual faith and "complete dependence on God"?
3. If a person wants to depend more fully on God, what might be the first step? The second?
4. Why is it imperative that a person initially come to God in brokenness?
5. What is the difference between earthly sorrow and godly sorrow?
6. Why is it important to first confess one's own sins, then also confess the sins of one's family and the general population?
7. What part does fear play in reverence?
8. What do prayer and meditation have to do with reverence for God?
9. How does reverence motivate a person?
10. Compared with God's people in Nehemiah's day when the Law was read, do we have more or less of a desire for the Word today?
11. What are the implications of the statement, "God has spoken"?
12. If a person does not have a thirst for God's Word, is there a way to develop that thirst?
13. Why is prayer vital to a leader of God's people?
14. Why must prayer be "frequent and passionate" in the life of a leader?

REBUILDING THE CITY OF GOD

15. Why do people often look for cleverness and business savvy in potential leaders, rather than a deep prayer life?
16. What does it mean to identify with God and His purposes?
17. Why is identification with God important?
18. What are some of God's purposes with which we ought to identify?
19. How important is it that a leader identify with God's people, as well as with God Himself?
20. How is "a passion for God's people" different from simply representing the interests of God's people?
21. What does it mean to passionately intercede for people?

3
CHARACTER

As we walk, people on the street stop to acknowledge the governor. Some bow in respect, while others wave and shout with enthusiastic smiles.

The scene is unusual. A few buildings are completed and occupied, while others are under construction. But there are still large areas that look like those old photographs of a devastated Europe after World War II.

"Yes," Governor Nehemiah is saying, "in my view, being a *spiritual* person is the first requirement for godly leadership. It overshadows all else. But there are other attributes that also are necessary, but which are not necessarily spiritual. They are characteristics that make a life noble and true. And they make up the second part of that *special kind* of person. Together they constitute **Character**."

We interrupt. "Sir, we think we understand what you mean by 'character.' But to be sure, would you give us an idea of the kinds of traits you include in that word?"

"Certainly," the governor responds. "In my opinion, character has to do with our reputation, to some extent, but especially it has to do with the moral excellence of our life. It is how we behave with others and how we treat them . . . and perhaps above all, it is how we behave when we are alone.

"The first trait that comes to mind as I think of character is really the key to living a noble life:

1.
A leader must recognize that humility unlocks knowledge and wisdom.

"I believe that God is able to more fully use the humble person, the person who has a correct view of self. Surely you have discovered that pride has ruined many, many leaders. King Saul, you may know, began as a humble servant, but he was lifted up with pride. Envy drove him mad — to the point that he became obsessed with killing the Lord's anointed, King David.

"If a person is proud, it is impossible to know true knowledge and wisdom. Pride chases away truth, because the proud person assumes that he or she already knows the truth. This is especially so with the wisdom of God. If a person is filled with self, there is no room for God's truth.

"As I speak of truth, another very important characteristic comes to mind. We find this principle in the Torah's story of the ancient Garden in Eden. There, we learn that the first man and woman lost their dominion over Paradise through *deception* . . . through the *lies* of the Serpent. People through the ages should have learned the tragedy of untruth, beginning with that disobedience and

CHARACTER

that Great Fall. But sadly we have not. Even among the greatest of our fathers, lying and deception were common and wrought terrible consequences.

"The lesson for us is, a leader's character must be an example for those who are called to follow. Such character demonstrates:

2.
A leader must trust that honesty is worth the pain and price.

"Think of how many people in the past who, when in jeopardy, could have saved their skins by lying. Especially, lying about their faith in God. Think of how many individuals there were who could have gained fortunes through dishonesty. Of course, there are countless examples of those who *did* save their lives and *did* gain their fortunes by lies. Thousands of them perished in the same waters that saved Noah, a man of truth.

"When I speak of honesty, I am not speaking of people who simply tell the truth *most* of the time — or all but a tiny portion of the time. Liars do that. Even they cannot live their lives outside the realm of truth most of the time. But liars are liars because they *cannot be depended upon* to tell the truth. *That* is what makes them liars.

"A leader must be trusted by the people. But only an honest leader is truly trusted. And sooner or later, every leader's life is proven true or false. People can usually smell a hypocrite at great distance."

REBUILDING THE CITY OF GOD

We walk a few paces in silence. We sense that the governor is deep in thought — or prayer. Finally, we break the silence and say, "To that attribute of honesty, Governor Nehemiah, may we add the kind of courage you have shown? You obviously are a courageous man. We have heard the stories of how you stood your ground against Sanballat, Tobiah, Geshem and all the other enemies of God's people."

"Well," replies the governor, "courage is an important attribute of a godly leader. But I hasten to say that it is a certain kind of courage. Think about the leaders in the past. They did not always run here and there doing brave things all day long! Their courage began in a small way. In other words:

3.
A leader must begin with the courage of one step.

"The courage of one step?" We are puzzled. "What does that mean, sir?"

Nehemiah explains, "The man or woman of God must have the courage to take only the first step toward some noble goal, trusting that the Lord will supply the courage, the power and the direction for the *next* step . . . and the *next* . . . to the hundredth step.

"Many who would be leaders seem to want to see far into the future. They want to know that they will succeed. But real courage is taking the first step because

CHARACTER

it is the right thing to do, whether success will come or not. I fear that I would have terribly failed if I had trusted in my own courage from start to finish. But I had just enough courage to take the *first* step — to confess my grief to King Artaxerxes — then God *gave me* the second step, and the third, and on to the finish.

"So long as my personal guards are around me, protecting me," the governor continued, "I am not afraid. But even more, is not God also my bodyguard, surrounding me continually with His power and presence when I am in His service? So another way of looking at courage is to say that the godly leader, who may give the appearance of being courageous, is simply trusting in God's overshadowing presence."

He thinks for a moment then adds, "As I speak of the courage of one step, let me tell you of the most *important step* that God wants all people, and especially leaders, to take:

4.
A leader must be a willing servant of people.

"The Lord does not require brilliant, attractive, talented or confident people. Instead, He needs only people who say with the prophet Samuel, 'Speak, for your servant is listening.' I *did not ask* to be governor of this city or the leader of the rebuilding of Jerusalem. I was simply a willing servant, and I obeyed God.

REBUILDING THE CITY OF GOD

"Our builders were not just carpenters and stonemasons; they were goldsmiths, perfume-makers, priests, Levites, administrators . . . all sorts of people. It gives me joy when I think that among the men who pushed and lifted and labored were the daughters of Shallum, young women working there beside their father, doing what they could to build the wall. All were needed. All were used by God. Because they were willing.

"The point is, in God's work we must not say, 'That is not my job.' In God's work, administrators may become stonemasons . . . and cupbearers," (he points to himself) "become administrators. We do what we are called to do, because we are *willing servants* of the God Most High."

We arrive at the outer courtyard of the Temple. And we stand looking up at the top of the Holy Place as it towers above the courtyard walls. Everyone is silent.

This building is a pale replica of Solomon's temple, of course, but in its own modest way, it is still awesome. In a little more than 400 years, Herod the Great will rebuild it in a grander fashion, then 90 years after that, the Romans will come and pull it down for good. Only the "Wailing Wall" will be left as a testimony to the great dwelling place of the Most High.

Nehemiah speaks quietly. "To love the Lord God and to love this place demonstrates a love for the Law and the Prophets also. And this is yet another attribute of the godly leader."

CHARACTER

After a few moments of silence, the governor returns to his discussion of character. "I will tell you another important trait of a noble person," he says, "and that is *patience* in well-doing. What exactly does that mean? It means:

5.
A leader must never give up.

"When my enemies — and even my friends — were telling me that I would die trying to rebuild this wall, I refused to listen. I was stubbornly faithful to my God and the vision He had given me.

"In my experience, I have noticed how quickly many people give up on their dreams. They seem to have little endurance. But we must be patient with ourselves and with our God. We must press on and not give up. When a godly leader has a mission to accomplish, there is only one direction he or she may go. Forward! Forward! Toward the goal!"

The governor's excited words hang in the air as we rapidly scribble on our pad again, listing the additional character trait that Nehemiah mentions.

The governor begins again. "Some perhaps will say that I am too intense or too narrow in my perspective. They will say that building the wall and removing the disgrace of the people is all I think about. They will say I am obsessed with that one goal. And I suppose that is true. However, I believe that a leader *must* be tightly focused. When a leader's mind is divided and consumed by too many concerns, effectiveness is lost.

6.
A leader must be single-minded.

"Single-mindedness speaks of dedication and commitment to a specific goal. It speaks of great energy and effort being channeled into a noble cause. It speaks of conviction concerning the worthiness of the mission.

"If the leader is not fully concentrating on the goal, how can the people be? The leader must be like the point of a spear: all the strength and force of the warrior, all the weight of the shaft and the spearhead are brought down to a single, sharp point. Power that is finely pointed — that is the secret of the spear . . . and of the godly leader."

We interrupt. "Sir, are you saying that the leader should not have other interests in life? That family and friends and things like recreation and enjoyment in living must be put aside?"

"No," replies Nehemiah. "That is not what I am saying. All those other things make a full and balanced life. What I am saying is that the leader's goal is always there, somewhere in the center of the mind. And when the leader daydreams or drifts off into deep thought, it is about serving people, about the mission and about God."

The air falls silent again as we ponder questions and answers. Though the governor might be described by

CHARACTER

some as "driven," he seems perfectly capable of savoring the silence, of just enjoying the company of newfound friends, without the need to constantly lecture or advise or posture himself as the expert or superior.

Finally, we say, "Governor, as you speak of single-mindedness, it occurs to us that God's leader also must be absolutely convinced of the goal — that thing on which the mind is so singularly focused."

"Certainly," replies Nehemiah. "But allow me to add something to that. There is no doubt that a leader must be fully convinced of the value of the mission. But in the midst of that single-mindedness, the leader must be ready to alter the mission or change it entirely if that is the will of God — or if it is perceived that God is opening a better way.

"Perhaps I can state it as a principle this way:

7.
A leader must be open to revising the mission.

"Although the godly leader should be *stubbornly* faithful to the Lord God and to the mission, stubbornness becomes a detriment when the leader is not open to change. Change is hardly ever easy or pleasant. But it is necessary. Because, whether we like it or not, to live is to change. Growth is change, and when we cease growing — physically, mentally, spiritually — we die.

"Seldom does God reveal His plan to us from start to finish. Usually He gives us only one part of the journey — and when we have obeyed, then He gives us another part. So, we always must be open to a new mission."

We are infected by the enthusiasm and excitement in Nehemiah's voice. We can see how the great leader would be capable of calling the Jews to action with those famous words, "You see the trouble we are in. . . . Come, let us rebuild the wall of Jerusalem, and we will no longer be in disgrace."

As we think of Nehemiah's inclusive language, a question occurs to us. "Sir, you always seem to include yourself with those who are or were in disgrace here in Jerusalem, with those who have sinned. Why do you do that?"

"It is very simple," answers the governor. "I include myself because *I am included* among those who have sinned. I am no different. Perhaps I have not failed at the exact same point as another, but believe me, I have failed. I mean no offense, but *so have you*. It is deadly for God's leaders to be lifted up with pride, to somehow conclude that they are different, that they are better, that they are not subject to the same rules and the same weaknesses as all others.

"Perhaps much of our success here in Jerusalem was due to the fact that I was always a leader *among* the people, rather than a leader *over* the people. Did you catch the significant difference between those ideas? Somehow the laborers always know the heart of the leader: if there is a secret feeling of superiority, they will sense it, they will know. So the leader must be humble and be of the same spirit as those who follow."

CHARACTER

We suggest, "It seems that many of the traits you have discussed might be summarized with the word 'integrity.' Do you agree?"

"Integrity?" Nehemiah says to himself out loud. "Yes, but that is a difficult word. Sometimes too difficult to really understand. But certainly the godly leader is a person of integrity. Perhaps integrity is the same as 'noble character.' Maybe we can say: *Noble character is wholeness, completeness, soundness . . . INTEGRITY.*

"Integrity is more than honesty or sincerity, you know. And yet, that is where it begins — with honesty. And the greatest test of honesty is whether or not we can tell ourselves the truth. As sinners, we sometimes lie to others or mislead them. But if we lie to ourselves, there is no hope for us. We soon are unable to tell right from wrong, light from darkness, reality from fantasy.

"Yes, integrity is a difficult word . . . and yet, it is a very wonderful idea. It goes beyond honesty to inner peace and, especially, soundness of soul. I believe one can be honest but still not be at peace with God and self. The picture I have of integrity is that of a person walking atop a very narrow wall. The wall is truth, the foundation upon which the person lives and moves. But the very act of walking along this narrow foundation calls for **balance** — balance in our thoughts, in our words and in our deeds; in compassion, practicality and insight; in relationships with family, fellows and God."

REBUILDING THE CITY OF GOD

Nehemiah motions in the direction from which we have come, toward his quarters. We all take one last look at the Temple and its courts, then slowly move on.

"In all of these traits," the governor says as we walk down the narrow street, "do not think that anyone can be so shrewd as to not need God. In my wisest moment, I am still but a child in understanding. Ah, but my God knows everything and sees everything! That is why I pray as I rise in the morning and as I lie down at night. It is why I prayed at that moment when I went before the king, and later as I surveyed the city, then as I called the people to the challenge, and as I moved around the city on my rounds. I pray always. It is my refuge against the Evil One, and *it is my strength to lead the people.* There really is no such thing as a great spiritual leader . . . there is only a great God Who moves in human hearts to accomplish His will."

We write in our notepad: *"In a godly leader, character is produced by a spiritual emphasis; outstanding character must have a spiritual source."*

Then we summarize Nehemiah's concepts by expressing the following principle:

CHARACTER

*The godly leader is a
"special kind of a person"
because of
spiritual qualities
and **noble character.***

REBUILDING THE CITY OF GOD

We are beginning to grasp something of Nehemiah's concepts of leadership. The governor is saying that godly leadership is based upon a *spiritual approach to life.* And this spiritual approach leads to the creation of a noble character — produces a person of integrity.

Now we are anxious to discover what Nehemiah means by "a special kind of plan."

CHARACTER

Reflections on What It Means to Be a *Special Kind of Person:*

The Character Component

1. What is the difference between knowledge and wisdom?
2. How does humility unlock knowledge and wisdom?
3. How will the lack of humility hinder a leader?
4. Can you think of examples of how or when honesty can be painful or costly?
5. If a person is honest most of the time, can he/she be considered "honest"? Why or why not?
6. How is honesty valued in our society today?
7. How cautious should a leader be?
8. Is there a relationship between courage and faith in God?
9. How much courage does a leader need?
10. Why are willing people more valuable to God than talented or brilliant people?
11. How do we develop a willing spirit?
12. Why is "servant of people" the *highest*, rather than the lowest, position which we can attain?
13. Why do people give up on their dreams?
14. Why or when should we be "patient with ourselves and with our God"?
15. How is endurance related to faith?
16. What happens to people who are double-minded rather than single-minded?
17. Can a single-minded person have a good family and healthy relationships?
18. How do we know if we are single-minded toward God?

REBUILDING THE CITY OF GOD

19. How can a person be faithful and single-minded and *also* be open to "revising the mission"?
20. Is change necessary? What kind?
21. How do we know when the mission needs to be revised or completely changed?

4
STRATEGY

When we arrive back at the governor's residence, Nehemiah orders a food tray brought into his private chamber. We sit on pillows, eating olives, goat cheese, and bread. And soon the general conversation returns to how the city has been rebuilt.

We say, "Sir, you said earlier that a leader must be 'a special kind of person with a special kind of plan.' You have explained what you mean by a *'special kind of person'* — a leader who has spiritual qualities and noble character. And now we hope you will teach us about the **special kind of plan** such a leader must create."

"Yes, of course," says Nehemiah, "I will be happy to tell you what I can — not that I am an expert, you understand.

"By the way, I find it interesting that everyone seems to have an opinion on how things should be administered. Many people think they themselves should be leaders. But before I came here to Jerusalem, no one stepped forward to lead the people who were in disgrace. If someone had, I would not have had to travel all the way from Persia.

REBUILDING THE CITY OF GOD

"Frankly, no one has even come to ask for my suggestions on leading God's people. No one but you. Hundreds have come wanting favors — privilege, power, honor — but none wants to know how to become a humble, godly leader. Maybe this is one of the reasons we tend to fall into disgrace.

"But back to your question. After one has become that certain kind of person of which I spoke — a spiritual person who has developed an honorable character — then it is time to develop a leadership plan. I have known spiritual people of integrity who never became real leaders because they had no plan . . . nor, apparently, even a thoughtful mission. So, God's leader must not only be godly, but also be a perceptive planner, with a clear vision of where to lead the people."

We have already opened our notepad, and we quickly write: Godly leadership involves **Strategy.**

Nehemiah continues. "I well remember the day I entered King Artaxerxes's presence after hearing about Jerusalem's plight. I believe I was prepared for whatever might happen. First, I had been praying and fasting for several days. I had *prepared myself spiritually* for that specific moment. But I also had prepared my mind with a plan . . . perhaps not in every detail, but I had a vision of where I wanted to go and what I wanted to do.

"The king said to me, 'What is it you want?' Again I prayed to my God, then I said, 'If it pleases the king and if your servant has found favor in his sight, let him send me to the city in Judah where my fathers are buried so that I can rebuild it.'

STRATEGY

"You see, I was prepared to put into words what I wanted to do. But let me hasten to say that it was not simply *my own desire* that gave me such boldness. I believe God laid it upon my heart to rebuild the city. He placed His vision within my mind and spirit."

"So," we interject, "you were prepared for the challenge because you had a specific vision that God had given to you?"

"Yes, but that is not all," the governor replies. "The king asked me specific questions concerning the plan, and I was prepared to answer those questions. He asked me how long the project would take, and when I would get back. I had thought in advance about that and was able to give him a satisfactory answer. While I was at it, I also asked him for letters of safe conduct to give to local officials of the regions through which I would travel. And also a letter to the keeper of the royal forest, so I might have wood for the gates and for this residence in which we now sit. All my wishes were granted by the king, because God's gracious hand was on me. In fact, the king even sent a company of cavalry with me, to protect me."

We think for a moment, then ask, "So you are saying that the key was God's gracious hand upon you?"

Nehemiah nodded, but added, "God's gracious hand . . . working through or with the plan *I was ready to offer.*"

We are impressed with the thoroughness of the governor. Nehemiah doesn't get caught up in minor details, but he does look ahead and prepare for sweeping, strategic contingencies. We write in our pad:

REBUILDING THE CITY OF GOD

1.
A leader receives the vision and develops the mission.

Nehemiah continues, "When I finally reached Jerusalem, I developed my plan further by collecting specific information and analyzing and evaluating it. I did nothing or said nothing concerning the plan for three days after arriving in the Holy City. Then, on the fourth day when darkness came, I mounted my horse, took a few guards with me and surveyed the city. I examined the wall by night because I didn't want the people to wonder what this stranger from Susa was doing in their midst.

"When all my research was done, when I had completed my plan and was finally ready, I called together the priests, the nobles, the officials and the people. I set a challenge before them: 'Come, let us rebuild the wall of Jerusalem,' I shouted, 'and we will no longer be in disgrace!'

"Then I told them about the gracious hand of God that was upon me, about how King Artaxerxes had given me leave to come here and rebuild the city. I think they were ready at last to commit themselves to the great rebuilding project . . . because they understood that I had created a plan. And furthermore, they believed that God really would help us succeed. And that is something to remember: If a leader expects people to follow, two things should be obvious to the people:

STRATEGY

2.
A leader has a well-conceived plan and has called upon God for His help.

"Both of these things are crucial, in my opinion. If one is missing, the direction will be unclear to some degree. But when the people perceive those two things, they are likely to shout, 'Let us start rebuilding.' When that happened here in Jerusalem, it was a powerful and emotional moment for me, as you can imagine."

"Excuse us, sir," we say. "Did your plans also include a way of dealing with Sanballat, Tobiah and the other enemies of the work?"

The governor's face hardens for a brief moment as he remembers all the deception and treachery of his enemies. Then he answers, "I did not know how devious and evil those scoundrels could or would be. But I suspected that the challenges would not go away. In fact, something told me that trouble would actually increase if we made progress and were successful. I suppose I sensed an important principle:

3.
A leader understands that, as work proceeds, opposition increases.

"And that is exactly what happened. The enemy first ridiculed us, then they tried to intimidate us. Next they tried to lure us into a trap, and finally they tried to blackmail us. As the wall reached higher, the enemy's deceit reached deeper.

"It was necessary for me to discipline my mind, if you will, so that I might lead the people in a *positive way*. But at the same time, I had to be on my guard against *negative influences,* both from the enemy and from within our own ranks."

We let all his thoughts settle into our mind, then we say, "Sir, we are impressed with your perceptions and vision. And that reminds us of the insights you had into the plots of your enemies. How did you gain such insights? Did God reveal them to you, or is that a natural instinct you possess?"

"Ah, a good question," Nehemiah smiles. "Let me first give you a rule — write this down:

4.
A leader must know who the enemy is, and, especially, who he is not.

"Now, you may think that statement goes without saying, but believe me, this is where many people go astray. Let me explain. During our work, some of the builders — poor people, ordinary people — came to me and told me that there were nobles and wealthy people who were charging them terrible interest on loans for their land and homes and crops. These rich people were so greedy that they were actually selling their own coun-

STRATEGY

trymen into slavery because those poor people could not pay their unjust debts. Can you imagine it? I was infuriated!

"Now, it would have been easy for me to conclude that these rich, greedy nobles were the enemy, and to treat them as such. But despite their deplorable behavior, they were my brothers and sisters! Sanballat, Tobiah, Geshem — *these* were my enemies. It was not difficult to recognize them.

"We often turn against our brothers and sisters, merely because we believe, or even know for sure, that they are wrong. Let me tell you, I dealt sharply with those ruthless people. I rebuked them and instructed them to stop their heartless behavior immediately. And they repented.

"So you see, people may be wrong, but they are not necessarily the enemy simply because they are in error. Most of the time, you will recognize the real enemy: he is the one who is working against you, not because he disagrees with your plan, but because he despises you, wishes you dead or gone, removed. He, in fact, is the instrument of the Evil One. So, know who your enemy is . . . and who he is not."

We speak up as Nehemiah pauses. "But once you identified your real enemy, how did you discover his plots? You seemed to see right through his schemes and his deceit. How did you know what evil he was planning?"

The great leader responds, "A moment ago, I mentioned that, as the work proceeds, opposition increases. Now let me go farther and say

5.
A leader must not be naive: Expect opposition, and post watchmen on the wall.

"Any good and noble work will be opposed by evil, either from without or within," Nehemiah continues. "If you think all is well, you do so at your own peril — and the peril of your people and your mission. It helps to do this exercise: Pretend you are the enemy, and ask, 'What should I do to confuse, frighten, discourage, intimidate, imbalance, or harm the work and the people of God?' Simply think like a human being — because we, as natural men and women, are wicked and devious creatures. It is not difficult to think like the enemy, because we ourselves sometimes behave as the enemies of God, as we sin against Him.

"But beyond that, post watchmen on the wall. Tell the people you trust that they must keep you informed, not only concerning flesh-and-blood enemies, but also concerning the phantom enemies — detrimental attitudes and influences — that loom on the horizon. Those watchmen may see discouragement and danger before you do, because your eye must remain on the mission.

"In fact, when any enemy poses a challenge, you must meet that challenge immediately. But do not dwell on it. Return right away to the work, because if the enemy can successfully distract you from your mission for a few hours here and a few hours there, your energy and enthusiasm may be diminished. That is such an important principle that I will state it this way:

STRATEGY

6.
A leader recognizes that *distraction* may be the enemy's greatest weapon.

"There are many shrewd techniques the enemy may use to destroy you or to prevent or harm the work of God done through you. So, the godly leader must be as perceptive as the enemy is cunning — and **identify the enemy's tactics.**

"The enemy always has an effective arsenal of weapons: ridicule, intimidation, insult, rumor, innuendo, blackmail, enticement, to name a few. But most of all, the enemy will try to create fear and discouragement in the hearts of God's builders. And fear is so irrational that it is often worse than the object or source of the fear."

We are puzzled. "We understand that a godly leader *should* identify the enemy's tactics. But we are not sure *how* to identify them. How did you recognize what your enemies were doing?"

"Usually that is not difficult," Nehemiah says. "For one thing, ask yourself, 'How am I being tempted to abandon the mission? Am I tempted to run away, hide my face in shame, turn aside from the work, compromise?' If I am tempted to do one of those things, then that is what my enemy wants me to do or *wants me to feel*. So I will refuse to respond as he wants and expects me to respond. In other words, if I feel fear, I have identified the enemy's tactic: he is trying to frighten me. Then I can do what I must do to remove the effectiveness of that tactic."

We say, "But how did you anticipate other tactics? For example, how did you know to set guards in the low places — or at other weak points along the wall?"

"You have answered your own question, my friends," says the governor. "If there is a point of vulnerability, count on your enemy to take advantage of it and attack you there. As I mentioned, this was my practice: I would say, 'Where are Nehemiah and his builders the weakest? Where and how can they be distracted or harmed?' When I answered those kinds of questions, I could then plan to defend myself and the workers. I believe it is the same in a spiritual battle with the Evil One and his demons. He attacks where we are weakest. So we must not deny our sinfulness and weaknesses, but be honest and admit those weaknesses — in order to fortify ourselves through God's power."

The room is quiet as we ponder the strategies of leadership. Finally, Nehemiah looks at us and says, "Most leaders are challenged to do more than they can possibly do. Perhaps you know that Jethro warned his son-in-law, Moses, that the great Lawgiver would wear himself out if he did not appoint leaders to assist him. With that in mind, here is another principle that was an important part of my planning: A leader depends on others to complete the work. Therefore

7.
A leader appoints helpers who are people of integrity.

STRATEGY

"For example, when the wall was completed, I put my brother Hanani in charge of security. I knew I could trust him with my life. I also appointed Hananiah to help my brother in supervising the safety of Jerusalem. I knew Hananiah was a man of integrity and a man who feared God more than most men do. I would suggest that you ***not*** appoint people to positions of importance just because they are your friends or are popular individuals. Integrity is vital. And equally important is their absolute respect and reverence for God. Perhaps in the nations of the world, you may have to play political games. But in the City of God, integrity and reverence mean everything."

The governor stands up and paces the room three or four times. Then he stops. "One other thing was crucial to my everyday leadership," he says slowly. "As time slipped by, it was necessary for me to remind the people — and myself — of our mission. Let me tell you, it is easy to be distracted in a hundred different directions: jealousies, arguments, differing objectives, lack of interest, fading confidence, fatigue, and on and on. So I say to you:

8.
A leader renews the mission daily.

"I assure you, in every work, great or small, you will be tempted to lose your concentration, your focus, your zeal . . . even your reason for embarking on the project in the first place.

REBUILDING THE CITY OF GOD

"I remember, early in the rebuilding, even the Jews who lived near our enemies came to us and told us over and over, 'Wherever you turn, they will attack us.' So I put some of the people behind the lowest points of the wall, as we mentioned earlier, at vulnerable places, and I assigned them to guard duty by families. Then I said to everyone, 'Don't be afraid of the enemy. Remember the Lord, who is great and awesome, and fight for your brothers, your sons and your daughters, your wives and your homes.'

"How easy it is to forget what we are really doing! We had to remind ourselves that we were not merely rebuilding a broken wall, we were repairing God's reputation — and our own. We were removing our disgrace. We were renewing our covenant with the God of the universe. And in all that, what was at stake? Our brothers! Our children! Our wives! The places where we live our lives!"

We continue to talk, hour after hour — questions and scribblings on one side, answers and memories on the other.

Finally, our mind toggles into overload, our eyes become increasingly blank and heavy. So the kindly governor suggests that we get some rest. We can talk again tomorrow.

But as we fight fatigue and lose, we know that in the morning, we must leave. We have an appointment with a window in time. And we cannot be late.

STRATEGY

Reflections on What It Means to Have a *Special Kind of Plan:*

The Strategy Component

1. How can a person be open to receiving a "vision" (purpose or goal) from God?
2. How can a person know that the impression (vision) is really from God?
3. Once a person truly has a vision, how should the mission be developed?
4. Do you think people will follow a leader who has a well-conceived plan and has called upon God for His help? Why or why not?
5. How will the people *know* that a leader has a plan and has called upon God?
6. What is entailed in "calling upon God for His help"?
7. Why does opposition increase as work becomes successful?
8. Where is opposition likely to originate? What means will it use?
9. "A leader understands that, as work proceeds, opposition increases." Why is it important to understand this principle?
10. How do we mistake people for the "real enemy"?
11. What is the result of mistaking people for the enemy?
12. Who is the "real enemy"? Are there accomplices?
13. Why will there always be opposition to good works?
14. What does it mean to "post watchmen on the wall"?
15. How does it help to "expect opposition"?
16. What are some of the distractions that the enemy uses on us?

REBUILDING THE CITY OF GOD

17. Why is distraction such an effective weapon?
18. How can we identify the enemy's tactics?
19. Are there other reasons why a leader should appoint helpers, beyond simply needing some assistance?
20. How can you recognize "helpers who are people of integrity"?
21. Why would anyone appoint helpers *other than* those of integrity?
22. "A leader renews the mission daily." How is this different from a previous principle that stated, "A leader must be open to revising the mission"?
23. How does one lose concentration, focus or zeal?
24. How does one renew that mission daily?

5
PROCESS

Nehemiah is used to rising early. As cupbearer to King Artaxerxes, he had responsibilities that called for him to be up and around by daybreak, overseeing the various chores of the royal household. And as interim governor of Jerusalem and its vicinity for the past several months, he has construction crews and security forces to manage. So, as is his custom, he pulls himself out of bed just before the first glow of sun warms the eastern sky.

However, when he walks into his central living chamber with a yawn, he is surprised to see his guests, already washed, groomed and dressed, seated where we were last night when we concluded our discussion.

We rise to our feet and extend our right hand. "Peace be to you, Governor Nehemiah," we say. "And thank you for your kind hospitality."

Grasping our hand, the governor replies, "You are most welcome. I trust you slept well. But why have you risen before the crowing of the cock?"

We smile. "Departure time is very soon, sir. We have a very long journey ahead of us. But we hope we may impose upon you for one more interview early this morning."

REBUILDING THE CITY OF GOD

"Certainly, you may," says Nehemiah. "It is a pleasure to visit with someone as enthusiastic about leading God's people as you."

"Thank you, sir," we respond. "Last evening, you indicated that a spiritual person who had developed a noble character was ready to accomplish two things. You said that the first thing was to develop a **plan,** what we in our country might call 'strategic thinking and planning.' But you did not mention the second thing. Would you speak about that for a short while before we must leave this morning?"

"I would be happy to do so," says the governor. Just then, an assistant appears in the door. Nehemiah asks the man to bring in some morning refreshments for himself and his guests. The man bows his head slightly and turns back into another part of the house.

"You have summarized my views well," continues Nehemiah. "The godly leader is indeed a person of *spirit* and *character,* a balance of virtues. But the leader also must combine an aptitude for planning — *strategy,* as you call it — with an aptitude for *applying principles in everyday situations.*"

We raise our hand slightly and say, "Sir, we think we know what you are saying. In our country, we might use the word 'process' as a way of saying 'applying principles in everyday situations.'"

"Very well," says Nehemiah. "We will say that the godly leader must join *strategy* with **Process.**

"Now, a person may be quite talented at planning — creating exciting and visionary ways of accomplishing a specific goal. Yet that same person may do poorly at

PROCESS

working through those plans in a practical, productive way. Likewise, someone may be excellent in completing tasks, getting them done well and on time. But that same person may be incapable of actually creating the plan or even conceiving a vision of any kind. Leadership, however, involves both things.

"We have talked of strategy, but to be balanced, we also must speak of . . . what did you call it? process? At least we can discuss some of the methods I used as we repaired the wall. To begin with, I decided that those who were former residents of Jerusalem should repair the wall in the area where they once had lived. They naturally would be interested in having the best possible protection for their own homes when the city was rebuilt. Since their future safety would depend upon their own skill and conscientiousness, they built the wall high and strong. I think it is a good rule and a practical process to follow:

1.
A leader realizes that people should build where they live.

"Now, that principle applies to more than building a wall. For example, we all should tend to the tasks that are close at hand, first. To care for our loved ones, to nurture or repair our close relationships, is superseded only by our obligation to God. In fact, though this may sound strange and even self-centered to you, a leader must be concerned for self above all others. I do not mean the leader should be preoccupied with personal comfort or safety before others. Rather, it is important to guard one's own faith and motives and character before endeavoring to lead or correct or teach others.

"And along with that, I believe it is more productive to work in family groups. There are many benefits from that working structure: it builds loyalty, responsibility, close ties, unshakable units. Beyond the family is the neighborhood, a collection of families. That is a natural way to group people in almost any task. And it is where I began in the building of the wall; I had the people work together as families and neighborhoods.

"Something else that is important to the work is mutual support. I assured the builders that they would not be left to face the enemy alone. Instead, when an attack came, a watchman was to blow the trumpet and others would come to the aid of those under assault. In order to build a wall or a house or anything else in this life, the worker needs *support* from brothers and sisters. Furthermore, I told those builders that help would be on its way quickly — we would *rush* to their side with support. And the Lord would be there, as well, to fight for us. So I say:

2.
A leader knows we must rush to the aid of those who need help.

"This is important because nothing is more discouraging than to work and strive, then find that you are alone

PROCESS

when danger comes, without anyone to strengthen your hands.

"Now let me mention a most important part of the process of building. No matter how much friendship, respect and love abounds among the builders, you can be assured that controversies will arise. It is natural, because we are human and we are sometimes proud, uncaring, overbearing and so on. I quickly learned that a significant part of my role as leader was to help settle disputes, to resolve problems."

We interrupt. "But sir, can you afford to delay the great and urgent work of rebuilding God's City to deal with petty squabbles, or even real and important issues? Could you not order the people to settle their own disputes?"

Nehemiah answers immediately. "Remember, my friends, that God's people always are doing more than building a wall. We also are building a spirit of unity and confidence. We are building relationships. Resolving conflict is not an interruption of leadership. *It is leadership!* Disputes impede everyone's progress, in addition to diverting our godly mission.

"When our people entered this ancient land by the hand of Yahweh, we had no king as did all the heathen nations around us. Instead, God set *judges* in Israel to resolve problems. No kings, only judges! There are times when people simply cannot move beyond their disagreements. In those cases, they need a wise and impartial person to help them solve their dispute and restore unity and brotherhood. So I suggest that you never forget that:

69

3.
A leader settles conflicts.

We feel compelled to object. "But sir, in our country, settling disputes requires special, extensive training. Do you think ordinary people can resolve conflicts without instruction from experts?"

Nehemiah shakes his head. "I believe a leader should have all the training available. And if one can be found who is specially schooled, use that person! But if that is not possible, the leader is not excused from the obligation of making peace. At least the godly leader can *try to help*. And I know success is not always guaranteed. But we can do our best, can we not? We must try. We must call together people of good will and help them reason with one another.

"But there is another situation that is similar to the previous one, yet involving a different process. I found that many of our people were not keeping God's Law in certain things. Remember, I told you that the rich were taking advantage of the poor. Now, I love to be loved — to be respected and admired — but it is not always possible to be subtle and mild. I discovered that I had no choice but to discipline those who were abandoning the instruction of the Lord. I had to decide that some actions were wrong; in other words,

4.
A leader confronts improper behavior.

PROCESS

"I'm not talking now about the kind of disputes we mentioned earlier, where answers are very difficult, where positions are taken and interests are deeply felt. No, I am talking about times when 'sin is in the camp,' and the leader must deal with it or the whole camp will suffer or be corrupted.

"That is not a comfortable task, if you have never had to do it. You feel quite inadequate . . . and timid. Who am I, I thought to myself, to scold or correct? But if the leader will not correct, then who will? People are not often self-correcting. A leader *must* call people back to God. If, in that process, the leader seems self-righteous, that is unfortunate — but it matters not. The leader *must* correct wrong behavior and call the builders back to the God to Whom they committed themselves."

We are busy writing in our notepad. When we pause and look up, the governor says, "These stone walls have a chill in them this morning. Come, let us move to the courtyard and warm our bones in the morning sun."

We rise and walk down the long hallway toward the bright entrance. We emerge into the early daylight, blinking and squinting. Nehemiah finds a bench and seats himself on one end. He gestures toward the other end, and we sit down as well. The sun immediately begins to soothe our stiff muscles.

The governor speaks again. "Part of the process is to *always be on your guard* — post watchmen, as I mentioned earlier. In addition, be on your guard especially when you meet with a victory, when you triumph. Does that sound strange? Believe me when I say that we are very vulnerable when we are celebrating. Remember this:

REBUILDING THE CITY OF GOD

5.
A leader understands that fear often follows triumph.

"Have you heard the story of Elijah's triumph? The great prophet, fresh with his amazing victory over the 450 prophets of Baal on Mount Carmel, was overcome with fear from the threat of one woman, Jezebel. You see, we become focused on our victory — we are successful and God is with us — and we think we are invincible. But the enemy strikes when we are overconfident.

"So, I determined not to be surprised by challenges and threats that follow on the heels of victory. I *expected* danger to press in on me, even while we were celebrating our accomplishments. And though I could not always ignore the fear in my heart, I refused to let it paralyze me. I tried to remember that triumphs are fleeting, while challenges are never-ending."

Nehemiah leans back so that the sunshine can bathe the sharp features of his face. He closes his eyes and soaks in the warmth. For a moment or two, his lips move in silent prayer.

Then he looks at us and continues. "I will give you one last process that was and is important to me, my friends. I call it 'setting things in order.' The godly leader may have many tasks to accomplish. In my situation, I had a very long and high wall to build — and gates and houses and buildings — a city, a people. So it was quite possible for me to be distracted from the most important goal, while attending to the many urgent details. But my God laid it on my heart to remind the people to *listen to Him,* to reexamine His Word, to recommit ourselves to a covenant of obedience. *These* are the truly necessary things, and this is the goal that is above all goals. Therefore, I urge you, as a godly leader to never forget:

6.
A leader sets things in order and calls for reform.

"Surely you have noticed the human pattern. Whether in spiritual things or in human affairs, we so easily lose our way. Our history is one of drifting away from our original direction, being called back by God's spokesmen, and finally being restored — only to repeat the process again and again. So, like a captain at the ship's helm, the leader must make constant corrections in order to maintain the course. Because of the sea's waves and currents, it is natural for the ship to drift, and it is unthinkable for the captain to tie the helm down, supposing that once he has set the course, he no longer needs to pay attention to the helm.

"Building Jerusalem — the City of God — is an outward thing, as are so many other tasks we undertake. But laying stone upon stone is only a figure, an illustration, of the more profound work we are doing, building precept upon precept into our lives. And building life upon life, person to person in love. So I say to you, listen to our God and renew the covenant of obedience to Him.

REBUILDING THE CITY OF GOD

Set these things in order, call the people to be reformed and restored . . . and you truly will be a *godly* leader."

We now have an idea of what Nehemiah meant by "a special kind of plan." We flip back in our notes to the principle we recorded earlier. Now we add the other part of Nehemiah's characterization of a leader. "The godly leader," we decide, "must not only have *spiritual qualities* and *noble character;* there is a second component that also is important to success." And we expressed the principle as follows:

PROCESS

*The godly leader has a
"special kind of plan"
that involves*
strategy *and* ***process.***

REBUILDING THE CITY OF GOD

We hold up our hand and say, "Governor Nehemiah, there is one last question. You have described to us a godly leader — whom you exemplify. But how many Nehemiahs are there? How often can we find someone who is a spiritual person with an honorable character, who also is a strategic thinker and planner, as well as a leader who can be counted on to work through a process to completion?"

Nehemiah replies, "A good question. And my answer is that there are more such people than you would imagine, because *God is at work* in the godly leader. But of these leadership traits, there are two that are absolutely necessary and cannot be overlooked: God's leader MUST be a spiritual person and a person of noble character. Beyond that, it is possible to form a partnership where a group of leaders pool their leadership resources. One leader may be a strong planner, another talented in working out a process in detail. I believe those qualities are necessary in the overall, collective leadership — but they may not be necessary in each and every leader. But every leader must contribute *something* to the partnership."

We glance at the position of the sun and know our time is running out. We look back at the great builder for a long time, studying the strength of character that shines through his eyes. We know we will never see Nehemiah again . . . until we meet in that future moment before God's Throne, when all the builders will gather to glorify the Creator.

PROCESS

Perhaps sensing our thoughts, Nehemiah says, "Before you leave, I will remind you of what I said earlier, of the greatest secret of our work for God, the secret of my success here in Jerusalem. It is prayer, my friends, *prayer!* A busy leader is always tempted to rely on himself and forget the true source of his power. The power is not in the builders or in their leader, but in the Lord. And prayer is the strong cord that binds us to Him, that keeps us from straying like a thoughtless ox.

"So do not forget to pray. Forget to savor your triumphs or boast of your victories. Forget to congratulate yourself. But *do not forget to pray to Yahweh.*"

We stand and extend our right hand again toward the governor. "You have honored us more than you can possibly know," we say through a tight throat.

Nehemiah ignores the outstretched hand, steps forward and embraces us. "Shalom, my friends," he says. "Go with God."

A guard opens the door to the courtyard, and we walk through. We glance over our shoulder in time to see the gracious governor raise a hand in farewell, then we turn and walk down the ancient street.

REBUILDING THE CITY OF GOD

Reflections on What It Means to Have a *Special Kind of Plan:*

The Process Component

1. "A leader realizes that people should build where they live." What is the spiritual application of this principle?
2. Why is it important to "build where they live"?
3. Why should a leader be concerned for self above all others in certain aspects?
4. Have you ever felt abandoned in a work? How did it feel?
5. Why is "rush" the operative word in this principle?
6. What kinds of situations can you imagine where people might need help, and need it quickly?
7. Why is it important to not ignore conflict?
8. Why is it the leader's obligation to try to settle conflicts?
9. Why did God originally give Israel judges rather than kings?
10. When there is a sinful situation, why is it important to deal with it rather than ignore it?
11. What happens if you don't deal with it?
12. What if you feel inadequate, unprepared or unqualified to deal with the problem?
13. What causes this phenomenon: "Fear often follows triumph"?
14. How are we vulnerable when we are celebrating success?
15. Analyze the story of Elijah's flight in the face of Jezebel's threats. What made him run?

PROCESS

16. In your experience, how often is reform needed?
17. Why do people drift away from their commitment to God?
18. What is entailed in "setting things in order"?

6
THE N FACTOR

Back in the countryside, we hike to the marked place where we entered this ancient world 24 hours earlier. We carefully uncover our vehicle and climb inside. And we wait.

The strong face of Governor Nehemiah forms in our mind. Concepts of leadership turn over and over in our thoughts. Suddenly, we are jerked from our contemplation by a distant roar. It grows louder and louder, coming from behind us.

As the sound reached nearly ear-splitting level, we are engulfed in blackness.

We open our eyes and blink. Now we can distinguish a voice saying, "Welcome back! You've succeeded . . . you are home!"

We are surrounded by medical and scientific monitoring equipment, and a television camera records every word and movement. We know we will be debriefed soon.

REBUILDING THE CITY OF GOD

But first we want to try to remember as much as possible.

We pick up our equipment pack and withdraw the notepad that we used in the interviews with Nehemiah. We glance over the quickly scribbled notes and decide to rewrite them and expand the thoughts while the impressions are fresh.

According to Nehemiah, we remember, A godly leader is a special kind of person with a special kind of plan. The *kind of person* is represented by the **Spiritual and Character Components** . . . a devoted leader with *spiritual qualities* and a developed *noble character.*

Nehemiah also believes, we remember, that the godly leader must be capable of creating a *special kind of plan,* represented by the **Strategy and Process Components** . . . developing *strategy,* then working through various *processes* to a successful conclusion.

All these leadership characteristics are things that need to be studied and incorporated into the lives of present and potential church leaders, we decide. We ourselves need to identify with God and increasingly become persons of integrity. We need to think strategically, not only in the professional world, but in the church as well. And we need to follow through on our mission, to work out the plan through a dynamic process.

We slowly examine our notes. At each entry and each rule, we stop to make present day applications and are amazed to find that every principle easily can be adapted to church situations we are aware of.

And yet . . . *something is missing. What is it?*

THE N FACTOR

We lean back and stare into nowhere. As we ponder, we begin to realize that there were other elements in Nehemiah's life and leadership that were overarching attitudes and approaches. There was an intangible quality, a special factor . . . the Nehemiah factor.

But what is this "N Factor," as we decide to call it? We try to stand back in our mind and see the panorama of Nehemiah's leadership.

As we had listened to Nehemiah, we had found ourselves thinking, "This man makes it clear that

(Factor 1)
There are only three types of people in the world: *Builders, Destroyers* and *Spectators*.

Of course, to Nehemiah, being a builder had nothing to do with architecture, engineering or the construction trades. He himself was a consummate builder, not necessarily of walls or buildings or cities. But of mission, unity, self-respect, hope. He was a builder of people.

A builder is someone who steps out and makes a difference, in a positive way, regardless of the field of endeavor. The things that are noble, helpful, uplifting, inspiring — the good things — these are the products of the builder.

The destroyer, on the other hand, sees good in nothing. Not only does the destroyer fail to make a posi-

REBUILDING THE CITY OF GOD

tive contribution to society, he or she actually tears away at its fabric in big and small ways. The destoyer fights against the builder, because he or she is bitter, angry, hateful, hopeless or cynical. Typically, he or she is also selfish, scheming, devious, or driven by power, possessions and prestige. The destroyer's goal is to win at all costs, to have it all — or to make everyone else as miserable as he or she is.

Spectators comprise the largest group. These are people, for the most part, who drift through life without a sense of calling or purpose. They simply sit and watch life's drama, the struggle between the builders and the destroyers, and try to understand it. They often are disengaged from the most meaningful things in life, and are primarily interested in getting along, having fun, being at ease.

Without the builders, we decide, this world would not be fit to live in. The path of least resistance has its appeal, of course; that's why there are so many spectators. It takes no talent, and there are no risks in just watching the action created by others. But thank God there are people who step out, who act, who build, who lead!

We think again about this man who has become even more of a hero to us. "What a remarkable person," we whispered. Then immediately, as if the thoughts were inextricably joined, we think, "But even more, what a truly awesome God he served."

THE N FACTOR

We hurriedly write in our notepad, "While Nehemiah was the greatest leader we have met, he never failed to call attention to the source of his power as a leader: God!" Part of the N Factor is never forgetting who the real hero is. Though Nehemiah lived a truly remarkable and heroic life, he illustrated the truth that

(Factor 2)
A godly leader's life points to God.

Our lives usually exhibit the source of our power, we decide. If people are overly-impressed with us as individuals — impressed with our intelligence, our cleverness, our talent — that may reveal the possibility that our power is human and earthly. But if people praise God because of us, it may be because they see that ours is a heavenly power and God is its source.

Suddenly we become philosophical. Precisely what was Nehemiah's task? we question. Surely, it wasn't building a wall . . . or building a city. He said he was building a people. But is there an even more basic way to express his task? Let's see . . . .

As we ponder, we say again, "Let's see . . . ." Suddenly a flash of insight comes. That's it! *To see.* Nehemiah saw things others didn't see!

REBUILDING THE CITY OF GOD

It is true. Nehemiah saw a city in disgrace — and himself and his fathers in disgrace — when many others apparently didn't. Though he had no experience in building even a small house, much less a city, he could see a strong wall and a restored city where people walked tall and little children learned the Torah. He could see God fighting an enemy and lifting up the hands of the builders. His was the vision of a deep and settled faith.

And that is part of the N Factor, we decide. In the final analysis

(Factor 3)
The true task of a godly leader is to see what others cannot or will not see.

We feel a sense of excitement. We are finally getting to the core — the Holy of Holies, if you will — of godly leadership.

Then perhaps the most profound thought regarding Nehemiah seizes us.

There was always a sense of calling in his thoughts, his speech, his actions, we remember. He was absolutely convinced that God had put a vision in his heart. He felt that he was commissioned, ordained. That he had a mandate. He pressed forward with every confidence because he was sure God was with him and would support and protect him. It was *his sense of calling* that empowered Nehemiah! A sense of calling that often is missing in would-be leaders today.

But there is something else, we are thinking. Nehemiah was not exhausted like so many conscientious leaders who nearly work themselves to death. He apparently understood that God had not called him to do all of the work (or even most of the work) himself — even if that were possible. He had the power and the will to motivate, delegate, appoint, enable.

Here's the point: Not only did Nehemiah know he was called by God, *he also knew his role was to call others.* The thought is exhilarating to us! That a human being would be *called* to cooperate in a mission with the King of the Universe is astounding. But then beyond that, that a human being would be called to participate in God's calling, to be commissioned by God to **call other builders** to the venture . . . what greater honor could there be?

We write the insight down and stare at it:

> (Factor 4)
> A leader is called, above all,
> in order to *call others!*

REBUILDING THE CITY OF GOD

We rest our head back again. It has been an exhausting, surprising, humbling . . . mind-boggling day and a half. Not only have we come face to face with a beloved and legendary person from ancient history, but we also have gained insights that will help improve our own spiritual leadership and the leadership of God's people in other places.

Spirit, character, strategy, process, we think. *The right kind of person with the right kind of plan.* Those principles, if embraced, could help us address the leadership crisis in many churches today.

Then our heart quickens as we think of the N Factor, and we mentally reviewed the Nehemiah principles:

It's crucial to know that (1) **builders are the ones who move the world** — they stand against the destroyers, and they challenge the spectators. Builders are godly leaders (2) **whose lives point to God,** rather than to themselves. And the true task of the builders is to have vision to (3) **see what others cannot or will not see.**

In the final analysis, we decide, builders are people whose agendas are set by God. Called by the Father to a special mission, they in turn (4) **call others to join in the crusade.**

A sense of our own calling quietly slips into our heart, even as our eyes grow heavy with fatigue. The pen falls from our hand, and the notepad slips to the floor. And in our dreams, we are walking once more with Governor Nehemiah in the shadow of God's Temple.

But somewhere in our dreams, we turn a corner and face the future.

THE N FACTOR

Reflections on the N Factor

1. Define a Builder, a Destroyer and a Spectator by describing people you know (but be careful not to disclose identities).
2. Sometimes it is easier to persuade a Destroyer to become a Builder than to persuade a Spectator to become a Builder. Why?
3. What are some of the "products" of the Builders?
4. What are the "sources" of many lives around you (what are people's lives based on)?
5. "Part of the N Factor is never forgetting who the real hero is." What does this statement mean?
6. What can we do if people are overly impressed with us as individuals (impressed with our intelligence, our cleverness or our talent)?
7. Is it pessimistic to see the disgrace of God's people when they go astray? Why or why not?
8. "The true task of a godly leader is to see what others cannot or will not see." How do you develop such powerful insight?
9. How does Factor 3 relate to the principle, "A leader identifies with God and His purposes"?
10. Why is it such a lofty idea that "a human being would be called to cooperate in a mission with the King of the universe"?
11. But why is it even more lofty to think that God has called us in order to call others?
12. How does a leader decide whom to call?

OUTLINE

I. *A special kind of person*
   A. The **Spirit** component
      1. A leader has complete dependence on God.
      2. A leader begins rebuilding broken walls by having a broken heart.
      3. A leader has deep reverence for God.
      4. A leader has a thirst for God's Word.
      5. A leader is faithful in communicating with God.
      6. A leader identifies with God and His purposes.
      7. A leader has a passion for God's people.
   B. The **Character** component
      1. A leader must recognize that humility unlocks knowledge and wisdom.
      2. A leader must trust that honesty is worth the pain and price.
      3. A leader must begin with the courage of one step.
      4. A leader must be a *willing* servant of people.
      5. A leader must never give up.
      6. A leader must be single-minded.

REBUILDING THE CITY OF GOD

      7. A leader must be open to revising the mission.

II. *A special kind of plan*
    A. The **Strategy** component
        1. A leader receives the vision and develops the mission.
        2. A leader has a *well-conceived plan* and has *called upon God* for His help.
        3. A leader understands that, as work proceeds, opposition increases.
        4. A leader must know who the enemy is, and, especially, who he is not.
        5. A leader must not be naive: Expect opposition, and post watchmen on the wall.
        6. A leader recognizes that *distraction* may be the enemy's greatest weapon.
        7. A leader *appoints helpers* who are people of integrity.
        8. A leader renews the mission daily.
    B. The **Process** component
        1. A leader realizes that people should build where they live.
        2. A leader knows we must rush to the aid of those who need help.
        3. A leader settles conflicts.
        4. A leader confronts improper behavior.
        5. A leader understands that fear often follows triumph.
        6. A leader sets things in order and calls for reform.

OUTLINE

III. **The N Factor**
   A. **Factor 1: There are only three types of people in the world:** *Builders, Destroyers* **and** *Spectators.*
   B. **Factor 2: A godly leader's life points to God.**
   C. **Factor 3: The true task of a godly leader is to see what others cannot or will not see.**
   D. **Factor 4: The leader is called, above all, in order to** *call others!*